SONS
OF GOD
ARISE

Sons of God, Arise

Copyright © 2016 Cleveland O. McLeish. All rights reserved.

No rights claimed for public domain material, all rights reserved. No parts of this publication may be reproduced, stored in any retrieval system, or transmitted in any form or by any means, electronic, mechanical, recording, or otherwise, without the prior written permission of the author. Violations may be subject to civil or criminal penalties.

ISBN: 978-1-63308-194-9 (paperback)

Interior Design by R'tor John D. Maghuyop

1028 S Bishop Avenue, Dept. 178
Rolla, MO 65401

Printed in United States of America

SONS OF GOD ARISE

CLEVELAND O. McLEISH

CHALFANT ECKERT

PUBLISHING

> *"Who Adam was before he sinned, is who you are now."*

I grew up believing that God went silent after the Bible was completed. How ignorant I was to think that our great God, who spoke life into existence, suddenly went mute for over 2,000 years. I realize now that He has been speaking all along. The problem is, we never learnt to listen. The results of not knowing the voice of the Lord have been catastrophic, and now the whole earth has plummeted into disarray. Confusion abounds in and out of the church, simple because we don't know what God is saying. The dividing line between truth and deception is not easily discernible by the average Christian. We don't know what God is doing or saying. Every Christian I know today is struggling to hear what God is saying in their particular situation. Even so, the spirit of religion propels us forward, and we continue our journey trying to figure it out as we go along, but lacking clarity and revelation that will help us walk specifically, and with the same purpose that perpetuated the life and ministry of Jesus. It takes great effort to learn to hear God, and it is only in knowing His voice that we are truly able to discern right from wrong.

> *But solid food is for the [spiritually] mature, whose senses are trained by practice to distinguish between what is morally good and what is evil.*
>
> –Hebrews 5:14 (AMP)

I began to train my senses to hear the Lord, and immediately He gave me an assignment. He said, *"Go for the lost, and heal the sick."* He also said, *"Preach and teach the Word."* How did I know that this was the Lord? It was commensurate with the definition of the church Jesus established.

St. Mark 16:16-20

"He that believeth and is baptized shall be saved, but he that believeth not shall

*be damned. And **these signs shall follow them that believe,** in my name shall they cast out devils; they shall speak with new tongues; they shall take up serpents; and if they drink any deadly thing, it shall not hurt them; they shall lay hands on the sick, and they shall recover. So then after the Lord had spoken unto them, he was received up into heaven, and sat on the right hand of God. And they went forth, and preached everywhere, the Lord working with them, and confirming the word with signs following. Amen."*

That was the last instruction Jesus left with the church before He ascended. In other words, "What I did, continue to do."

I like the fact that this scripture ended with amen. Amen means *so be it*. In other words, do not alter or change this meaning.

Jesus' assignment was carried on by the Disciples, Apostles, the early church, right to the end of the Bible, but somewhere in the history of the church's existence, we lost our way.

We once again became a religious institution built on traditions, rituals, programs and activities carried out through human intuition and effort and had no reliance or help from the Holy Spirit. In other words, we became the same church that Jesus challenged back in His day: The same church that met His actions with scepticism and doubt; the same church that tried to throw Him off the brow of a hill; the same church with demon-possessed people sitting in the pews, singing hymns, praying religiously, and teaching from the old covenant, but having absolutely no power or authority. It is now, hearing God, that I begin to see the relevance of this prophetic scripture:

Isaiah 60:1-2 (AMP):

"Arise [from spiritual depression to a new life], shine [be radiant with the glory and brilliance of the Lord]; for your light has come, And the glory and brilliance of the Lord has risen upon you. "For in fact, darkness will cover the earth and deep darkness will cover the peoples; But the Lord

will rise upon you [Jerusalem] and His glory and brilliance will be seen on you."

Everyone I know is sick or on medication for something. Cancer is spreading across this earth like an epidemic.

In recent times, Jamaica experienced what was known as a Chick-V Virus, which spread across the country rapidly like a cloak of darkness, then dissipated just as quickly. Caused by mosquito bites, no one knows where it came from, or where it went.

Almost everybody I know is struggling financially. Darkness is literally covering the earth and the people of the earth.

There was one time in history that One Man stood against this darkness and prevailed. His Name was and is Jesus Christ (Yeshua in Hebrew). He overcame the world, the devil and flesh.

His plan was to raise up a generation of people, without fear, who would walk in the same power and authority that He did, so He sent His Spirit to live in believers, and we have carried all that Jesus did for centuries inside us, but have never quite accomplished the same things He did, which is very interesting because He says:

> ...anyone who believes in Me [as Savior] will also do the things that I do; and he will do even greater things than these [in extent and outreach]...
>
> –St. John 14:12 (AMP)

This is what I want to challenge you as a believer with now. Jesus says we will do what He did, and even greater things. Yet it says in St. John 21:25, *"Jesus did many other things as well. If every one of them were written down, I suppose that even the whole world would not have room for the books that would be written."* If all that Jesus did was not recorded, how are we to know what He did, so we can do the same things, and even greater? St. John 16:14 gives us the answer. Jesus was speaking of the Holy Spirit when He said, *"...for he shall receive of mine, and shall shew it unto you."*

It is possible, like Jesus, for every born again Believer to *"...do only what he sees his Father doing, because whatever the Father does the Son also does." (St. John 5:19)* Until we get to that place,

> *The creation waits in eager expectation for the revelation of the sons of God.*
>
> –Romans 8:29

We are gates and doors that heaven passes through to the earth. If that entryway is blocked for whatever reason, the earth has a serious problem, which they do presently. Comparing the church then, to what it is now, is fascinating. We as believers have to make a choice as to which model is relevant. Do we settle for what it is now, or do we see the Biblical model more relevant, though there is no experience, proof or evidence that it is? I began to see the church, and the people for who and what it and they should be, and not what it and they are. The Lord then spoke to my spirit:

> *"You have been walking in a Prophetic anointing without even realizing it."*

That caught me by surprise, but I am beginning to see what is not, as though it is. I see people for who they really are in Christ, and that is prophetic. I see a glorious church, with men and woman walking this earth in the same anointing, same power, same authority, the very same likeness as Yeshua (Jesus). That is what I see, and I can't get around it. The Lord has been burning religion out of my system. I can't stand religion, but the only thing that can conquer the spirit of religion and witchcraft operating in our church today is the authentic power of God. We must walk in the supernatural power of the living God.

No more *playing* church. No more *doing* church. No more 'having a form of godliness, but denying the power thereof.' No more structure. What we need is a move of the Spirit, and this will happen when we begin to hear God and obey His instructions. The living Word must become our living reality. It must be what people see. When you look up from the pages of your Bible, you must be able to see what you just read.

The church started to change almost immediately after Christ left, and Paul spent a lot of time just trying to get people back to the original model of the church. He even spoke against 'other doctrines.' He said, even if an angel brought another doctrine, let him be accursed of God.

Today, we have learnt to have church without God. The Holy Spirit is not allowed to take over. The church has somehow become a part of the world system. We have compromised. People are having sex before marriage. The family altar has been destroyed. Christians are not spending time in the Word, or in prayer and fasting. We have settled for a powerless existence while darkness is spreading, and consuming everything in its path including our family, our finances, our health and wellbeing, and our peace and joy. We live today as if Jesus suffered and died in vain. Can you see the trademark of the enemy on our present existence? We get sick, and our first thought is a doctor. We get broke, and our first thought is to take a loan.

> *But seek first his kingdom and his righteousness, and all these things will be given to you as well.*
>
> –St. Matthew 6:33

We have replaced faith with reason and intellect; we have prioritized programs and activities over a move of the Holy Spirit; our Bibles have been replaced by cell phones. We lost our identity as a church, as children of God … but the Lord is restoring all that was lost, or stolen, through people all over the world who are not afraid of people's faces, not afraid of what people think, not afraid of change and not afraid of truth.

When we preach, the Bible says, the Lord will confirm His Word with signs following. We have lost that. We stopped preaching the Word and started feeding God's sheep with personal opinions, and private interpretations. God is changing that. If this is God's Word, I pray He will confirm it in your own life.

> *I hear the Lord saying, "I am going to raise up a Prophet among my people."*

When God gave me the assignment to 'Go for the lost, and heal the sick', I realized that I knew very little about reaching the lost and healing the sick. This was never something I practiced as a Christian. So, I had to study.

I have watched hundreds of videos from people all over the world, to see what God is doing through ordinary people like you and me. And amazingly, God has connected me with people locally and abroad who are walking in the supernatural. I have lost count of how many books I have read, but I had a lot of misconceptions that God had to deal with. I also had an issue with faith. I thought I had faith. God showed me, practically, that I had greater faith in the enemy and what the enemy can do than in God, and what God can do. This is the reality for most of us. If I asked you if you had faith in God, you would undoubtedly say, "Yes." If I asked if you struggled with fear, you would also probably say, "Yes." Fear is faith in the enemy. For example, if you fear death, then you really don't believe that God came to give you life. If you fear sickness, then you really don't believe that *By His stripes, you are healed*. If you fear calamity, then you really don't believe that God will give His angels charge over you. What you believe, you will receive. So, I dare to ask you again: **Do you believe God?**

God is original. The enemy counterfeits. If you are not careful, you surrender what is original because of the counterfeit. As a church, we are often guilty of this. The mere mention of prophets in church provokes different, often negative and sceptical, remarks from the leaders in the church. We fear prophets, because of false prophets. Yes, in the last days there will be many wolves in sheep's clothing, many false teachers and prophets who will perform all kinds of signs and miracles. If you can't tell the difference between what is authentic and what is not, you are already in trouble. It is not good enough to shun the gift of prophecy because of fear of the counterfeit. We must learn to differentiate between Moses' snake on the ground, and Pharaoh's snake.

There's a call for the sons of God to arise in this era. We were sent to earth in this time, for this season, and for this purpose. We must contend for what is ours, and never give up. God is calling for His sons and daughters on this earth to arise. This is your hour. This is your season. This is your time. God needs our co-operation for His power to manifest on earth. God rules in the heavens. Man rules on the earth, and it has been our responsibility from the beginning. We are the reason the enemy is wreaking havoc in our society. We are also the solution. We were created and fashioned in the same likeness and image of our Father, to subdue the earth and have dominion over it. We need to understand the place that we occupy on earth, and how we have blocked what God wants to do in the lives of people, maybe even in our own lives.

Jesus' life was one of power and miracles, but because of how the Bible is written, we have to take the time to rightly divide the Word of truth. If not, we would think, by just reading, that the concept of miracles must take place without our participation. That is a misconception. We have a part to play in what God wants to do in our own lives and the lives of others. We must rule the earth with His power, with His authority. David spoke to the giant with these words, "I come to you in the Name of the Lord."

Jesus got immediate results, but there are some principles that we miss so we do not see the results He saw. Jesus is the giver. Everything we need comes from Him. Everything you need, everything the world needs right now from God has already been paid for. 'Jesus paid it all' is not a cliché. It is a fact. When He said, "It is finished!" there was no but!

We are the receivers of what Jesus Christ paid for, but obedience is an element that stands between the giver and the receiver. If we miss that, what God gives will not reach to us. Jesus says, "If you love me, do what I say."

The problem we have as a church is not lack. We have a receiving problem. We easily accept our identity as born-again Christians but struggle to receive our identity as sons and daughters of God who can do the same things Jesus did.

If you have never been sick or never been broke, you might not easily grasp this, but you will when someone you know gets sick or finds themself in a position for which no human intervention can remedy. I know what it is to have a condition that baffles doctors. I know what it is to have financial institutions threatening to come and take away everything

I have. I know what it is to not have a car, not have enough money to provide for my family, and to not feel strong enough to make it through the day. I know what it is to cry, be tormented and oppressed, to be sorry I was born and want just to go to bed and not wake up. I know disappointment, frustration, ridicule and fear. I know what it feels like not to belong or fit in. I have even attempted suicide in the past to escape the pain in my heart. I have been hurt, wounded, embarrassed, ridiculed, laughed at, cast aside, rejected and crushed more times than I can count, but none of these things determines or influences what I believe anymore, because I choose, regardless of my circumstances to stand on the Word of God. I base my faith on God's spoken Word, and not on my circumstances, inadequacies, weaknesses or experiences.

> *"Beloved, I wish above all things that thou mayest prosper and be in health, even as thy soul prospereth."*
>
> –3 John 1:2

I contend for what is mine. I am a son, not a slave, and not a servant. Everything that belongs to Jesus belongs to me. I am joint heir with Jesus Christ. I was born to rule, born to have dominion, born to walk in the fullness of who Christ is. I am much more than just a human being. I was a spirit, a son of God before I was conceived.

> *"Before I formed you in the womb*
> *I knew you, before you were born*
> *I set you apart; I appointed you*
> *as a prophet to the nations."*
>
> – Jeremiah 1:5

I am learning that the Bible is more literal than it is symbolic. Religion will oppose that statement, but it cannot refute it.

I thought miracles could happen without my participation, without my input. The Lord said to me, "Look again!" I turned to the book of John, an excellent book on the life of Jesus, and I took another look and another look.

From what I know, there is no one on earth today who prays for people and sees 100% results as Jesus did. Jesus healed all who were sick and oppressed. I find that there are some people stronger in some areas than others; some are good with generational issues, others in spiritual warfare, others in counselling, others with pain, others with cancer, but God showed me a common denominator that is the key to seeing the same results as Jesus, the Disciples and Apostles. If we get this principle, it can change lives.

In St. John 2, Jesus and his disciples were invited to a wedding. His mother, Mary, was there. The wine ran out. Mary came to Jesus and said, *"They have no wine."* That is a message in itself. Jesus has what we need. If you lack anything, go to Jesus. Jesus responded to her, "My hour is not yet come." Mary turned from Jesus to the servants and said, "Whatever he tells you to do, do it." Those were the last recorded words in the Bible spoken by Mary. That is the key to our breakthrough. Whatever Jesus tells you to do, do it. That is your mandate as a son and daughter.

There were six big water pots at the wedding. Jesus told the servants "Fill them with water." They did it. Jesus then said, "Take some and carry it to the governor of the feast." Think about it, there is nothing normal or easy about that scenario. Personally, if I had been one of the servants, I would have need several preconceived reasons to tell the Governor of the feast as to why I brought him a cup of water. As far as I would have been concerned, what was in those jars was water. We don't see miracles because we would never take that cup of water to the man. We would never participate in such an activity.

If we missed the instruction or fail to carry it out, we miss the miracle. That is how easy it is to miss what God has for us. If we stop to think about it, we might choose not to follow the instruction. Our reluctance to participate blocks the miracle. Everything that Jesus wants to do on this earth today has to flow through our willingness to obey and participate.

In St. Matthew 14, five thousand men, not counting women and children, were sitting before Jesus and evening was approaching. The Disciples told Jesus to send the crowd away so they can get food. Jesus said, "No, you give them something to eat." Seriously, Jesus? Give them from what? Peter said, "We only have five loaves of bread and two little fishes." In John, one Disciple said, "We would have to work for six months to buy enough bread so each person could get one bite." Jesus took what they had, and blessed it, and broke the loaves. He then gave to the Disciples to give to the people. Jesus gives, but in order to receive we must be willing to participate. The Disciples were given the responsibility to distribute five loaves and two fishes to 5,000 men. Scripture doesn't suggest that the food multiplied before it was distributed. It could very well have multiplied while being distributed.

On many occasions Scripture records that throughout Jesus' ministry, those who received their miracle had to do something: take up your bed and walk, get up, go wash in the pool, go show yourself to the priest. Very often what they were asked to do looked extremely foolish. God will use foolishness to confound the wise.

There is a desperate need in the body of Christ for God's children to learn to hear Him when He speaks, so when the instruction comes, they know what to do. This is the key to manifestations of God's glory and presence. Very soon, hearing God will become a matter of life and death; wealth and prosperity; and sickness and health for every believer.

Without your participation, you receive nothing. It is yours. Contend for it. Healing is the children's bread. Are you a child of God? Don't give up. Whatever your needs are, God is willing to supply. Ask and you shall receive. Listen for the instruction, and do whatever Jesus tells you to do.

God is not a man that He should lie. (Numbers 23:19) If God says it, He will perform it. He watches over His Word to perform it. (Jeremiah 1:12) All His promises are yes and amen. (2 Corinthians 1:20) Everything is in place, and just waiting for the sons of God to arise in the earth, and take their rightful place, *seated in heavenly places with Christ.*

Moses and the Israelites were standing at the Red Sea with mountains on two sides. In the natural, the only logical way to go was to turn back. (Exodus 14) To eliminate that choice, God sent the enemies in pursuit behind them. There was really no turning back, but where else were they to go?

Sometimes problems come to push you in the right direction. Maybe everybody around you is getting sick and dying because God wants you to see that you can do something about it. Maybe demons are terrorizing those around you because God wants you to see that you can do something about it.

How often have we asked, "Where is God?" Where is the God of the Bible? Why aren't people being healed, and being set free from demons? Why are we not seeing any supernatural intervention in our lives, and the lives of those around us? I watched my father die from cancer, as helpless as can be. Where was the God of the Bible who healed? I know exactly where He was. He was lying dormant in me. We keep expecting God to come when He is already here. We have the Holy Spirit. We have the gifts of the Spirit. We are armoured and fully endowed with mighty spiritual weapons. We have everything we need.

If we refuse to participate in what God is doing, what He gives will not be received. The people started to complain to Moses, "Why didn't you leave us in Egypt?" Moses replied, "Stand still. Don't be afraid. The Lord will fight for you." Moses' focus was on defeating the army behind them. God says, "Why are you crying out to me? Tell the people to move on (forward)." Moses wondered, "Move on to where?" I hear Moses asking, "Don't you see the sea, God?" Then God says, "What is in your hands? Stretch out your rod over the sea."

Moses stretched out his rod. Now in the movies, with all the background music and dramatic expressions, that might seem cool. However, it must have felt very strange for one man just to stand up, and face the Red Sea with his hand in the air, while millions of disgruntled people were behind him filled with anguish and fear at the impending massacre, and Pharaoh's whole army closing in behind them. Nowhere to go. No experience in war. No hope. Here an 80-year-old man stands on a small ledge holding up a stick. This is a crazy and confusing scene, until that moment when the waters begin to shift by an invisible intervention. Look at God!

God, don't you see that the people around me are sick, and need healing? "Son, what is in your hand?" God, don't you see how financially bound I am? I never have enough food for my family. I can't afford the children's school fees. "Son, what is in your hand?" God, look how oppressed the young people are. They are addicted to drugs, pornography, masturbation, promiscuity and sex. They can't seem to help themselves, God, don't you see? "Son, what is in your hand?"

Jesus has sent us out into the world. He says, "As you go, proclaim this message: 'The Kingdom of heaven has come near.' Heal the sick, raise the dead, and cleanse those who have leprosy, drive out demons. Freely you have received; freely give." If Jesus tells you to heal the sick, raise the dead, cleanse the lepers and drive out demons, why aren't you doing it? You do not see it because you are not doing it.

> *"I hear the Spirit of the Lord say, become the answer you seek."*

The same Spirit that rose Christ from the dead, and enabled Him to walk in miracles, is living inside you. Do you really have a good excuse? Moses used a rod. You have the Spirit. You carry the fullness of who God is inside you, and you will be held responsible.

Jesus has issued some instructions to His church. He is waiting for us to obey and participate. We are not the ones waiting for God. The whole creation is waiting for the sons of God to be revealed.

I want to activate and initiate you in a practical course that will last for the rest of your life. You graduate from this course when you die. Every born-again believer is a perfect candidate for scholarship, and the only qualification is death to self. You pay daily.

Some of the things in the curriculum include, and these are the things that you can do:

- ✓ John 2 – *Turn water to wine*
- ✓ Mark 1 – *Drive out evil spirits*
- ✓ Matthew 8 – *Heal your mothe-in-law from a high fever*
- ✓ Luke 4 – *Heal many who are sick in the evening*
- ✓ Luke 5 – *Catch fish where there is no fish*
- ✓ Matthew 8 – *Cleanse a man from leprosy*
- ✓ Mark 2 – *Heal a paralytic*
- ✓ Mark 3 – *Heal a man with withered hand*
- ✓ Luke 7 – *Raise a widow's son from the dead*
- ✓ Matthew 8 – *Calm a storm*
- ✓ Mark 5 – *Cast demons into pigs*
- ✓ Matthew 9 – *Heal a woman in a crowd*
- ✓ Matthew 9 – *Heal the blind*
- ✓ Matthew 9 – *Heal the dumb*
- ✓ John 5 – *Heal an invalid*

- ✓ Matthew 14 – *Feed five thousand with a box lunch*
- ✓ Matthew 14 – *Walk on water*
- ✓ Matthew 17 – *Deliver a boy from demons*
- ✓ Matthew 17 – *Pay your taxes from a fish's mouth*
- ✓ Luke 13 – *Heal a crippled woman*
- ✓ Luke 14 – *Heal a man with dropsy*
- ✓ John 11 – *Raise a dead man after four days*
- ✓ Matthew 21 – *Speak to a fig tree and cause it to die*
- ✓ Luke 22 – *Heal a severed ear.*

This is just what was recorded. According to John, there is a myriad of other things Jesus did that was not recorded. The Holy Spirit will advise you accordingly. You will be instructed by Him, and the seven Spirits that stand before the throne of God:

> *And the Spirit of the LORD shall rest upon him, the Spirit of wisdom and understanding, the Spirit of counsel and might, the Spirit of knowledge and of the fear of the LORD - Isaiah 11:2*

Jesus says, *"Whoever believes in me will do the works I have been doing, and they will do even greater things than these, because I am going to the Father."* (John 14:12)

I declare that this is the *greater works* generation. The Church of the living God will rise up and be identified as God's Children. God will be a wall of fire around us and the glory within us. (Zechariah 2:5). This will be the generation that prays for the sick, and sees them recover. This will be the generation that will set people free from demons. We will not be afraid of the gifts of the Spirit. This will be the generation that masters sin. We will set precedence as God's righteous people in the earth. Everywhere our feet touch we will reclaim for God. Everything that has been stolen will be returned. We will not agree with poverty. We will not agree with sickness. Jesus took our infirmities and bore our diseases. This is the generation that will leave an inheritance for our children's children.

Faith will replace reason and intellect. The Holy Spirit will be elevated above programs and activities. The rule of God will be established in this house.

For generations, the enemy's agenda has been making the headlines in the media. I declare that the glory of God will make headlines:

Blind Man Healed
Man Born Lame Walks
Cancer Healed

The world is falling apart. The true sons of God are being revealed all over the world. Why not here? This is happening all over the world. It is going to happen here. This is not random; this is prophetic Habakkuk 2:14 says, *"For as the waters fill the sea, the earth will be filled with an awareness of the glory of the Lord."*

The glory of God belongs to His church. Contend for it, it belongs to you! You have what this world needs, established and living inside you. Don't deny them what you have.

Sons of God. Daughters of God. Arise, and shine. For the glory of the Lord has risen upon you. This is your time to shine.

Note from the Publisher

Are you a first time author?

Not sure how to proceed to get your book published?
Want to keep all your rights and all your royalties?
Want it to look as good as a Top 10 publisher?
Need help with editing, layout, cover design?
Want it out there selling in 90 days or less?

Visit our website for some exciting new options!

www.chalfant-eckert-publishing.com

www.ingramcontent.com/pod-product-compliance
Lightning Source LLC
Chambersburg PA
CBHW052045070526
44584CB00018B/2624